Dear God, I'm Letting Go

31 Days of Letting Go and Letting God

By Jasmine Cooper

Introduction

Letting go of something is never really easy, especially if you have grown attached to certain things. We all come to a point where God wants us to let go of something in our lives. Think about the story in Joshua 4 of the children of Israel who were to pick up 12 stones by the Jordan as they crossed over and leave them at a place called Gilgal, which means "separation!" They were to separate from some things so that God could do what He was going to do in their lives on their journey to possess the promise land. Letting go is, in a sense, saying, "I must part from you here, because it's time for me to move forward." This can be difficult because moving forward can bring change. Change is good! With change, however, comes new challenges, but new challenges bring new growth. I therefore encourage you to take this 31 Days of Letting Go and Letting God Challenge!

Let Go Let God Challenge Day 1: Starting Over!

Today is day one of letting go and letting God! You have been struggling for so long. We all took a big loss! We can let go together so that God can heal us, heal those around us, heal the situation, or do whatever it is He wants to do in our lives. We took a hard hit; now it's time to get back up! Today, I challenge you to let go and let God; give your issue to God. I know it's hard, but we can do this. We always feel like life is over when things come tumbling down, and then we don't even know where to start.

Challenge: Write a list of things you want to accomplish in the next 30 days to bring you to the next place in your life. We can live! If you have no goal, pray about it and ask God what He would have you do. Maybe it's to go apply for that job, or maybe to go spend time with an old friend, or perhaps a task you been putting off for a while; whatever it is, it's time to get back up and let God take control of your situation!

—Proverbs 29:18—

"Where there is no vision, the people perish: but he that keepeth the law, happy is he."

Let Go Let God Day 2: Rest

Relax. Get some rest! You have been doing way too much. So often we want to have control in the situations in our lives. We say we really rest in and trust God with our situations, but do we really? God has your situation under control. If you say you are letting go and letting God, then let Him work it out for you!

Challenge: Today, get some rest—real rest, not the rest where you say you're going to rest and end up doing a million things. Get the rest that eases your mind, body, and soul!

—Matthew 11:28-30—

"Come unto me, all ye that labor and are heavy laden, and I will give you rest. Take my yoke upon you, and learn of me; for I am meek and lowly in heart: and ye shall find rest unto your souls. For my yoke is easy, and my burden is light."

Let Go Let God Day 3: Let Go

You can't let go and let God if you don't *let go*. What are you still holding on to that you haven't given to God? The key to letting go and letting God is allowing God to be in control. The issue for so many people is that if they can't have control in one area of their lives, they will try to take control in another. You have to let go and let God have complete control of what He is doing in your life. Think about Peter as he walked on water. He had no control; he was just trusting completely in the Lord. Just remember—the second you start to doubt, you start to sink.

Challenge: Today, take that step of faith and let go completely!

—Hebrews 11:1—

"Now faith is the substance of things hoped for, the evidence of things not seen."

Let Go Let God Day 4: Only For a Season

Some things are only in your life for a season. It's unhealthy to hold on to people, jobs, homes and locations that were only meant to be in your life temporarily. We often try to make seasonal places in our life permanent, but you can't hold on to summer if it's about to be fall. You have to let the seasons change. It can be hard to let go of those places, people, or even things, but that doesn't mean God doesn't have a plan for your life. What was lost in the last season will be replaced in the next.

Challenge: Today, let go of what God needs you to let go of to move forward, whether it be friends, family, job, home, school or a situation. Whatever it is God wants you to let go of, let go of it!

—Ecclesiastes 3:1—

"To everything there is a season, and a time to every purpose under the heavens."

Let Go Let God Day 5: Trusting God

Letting go can be so hard, especially if it's the ones you love. You seem to toss and turn at night. Your tears seem to like waterfalls as you wrestle with God.

"Lord, bring them back. I miss them. Are they okay? Why did they have to leave?"

Know that God has a purpose and a plan, and His plan is bigger than you! So often, it hurts us because we take what happens so personally, and it becomes about us.

You have faith for everyone else's situations, but with your situation you feel there is no way. Your bills are starting to pile up, your kids are running wild, you keep arguing with your husband, and nothing is going right. You may cry some nights, you may worry some days, you may not understand why, but trust God.

Challenge: Ask yourself—do you really trust God? If you don't, today's the day to start trusting in the Lord. You may not be able to get a hold of your situation, but God can!

—Proverbs 3:5-6—

"Trust in the Lord with all thine heart; and lean not unto thine own understanding. In all thy ways acknowledge him, and he shall direct thy paths."

Let Go Let God Day 6: Forgiveness

Easier said than done! So many people say, *"Forgive but never forget."* Jesus doesn't live like that; He forgives *and* forgets. He pardons us from our sins and covers them with His blood. God gives us new mercies every morning, so why don't we live each day looking at the people in front of us like they never hurt us before, as though you just met them for the first time? Let go and let God heal you from the hurt they've caused you. I know it's hard, and I know they may never apologize, but forgiveness is not for them; it's for you!

Challenge: Let God heal you as you forgive. Don't repay evil for evil; rather, let God fight the battle for you!

—Matthew 6:14-15—

"For if you forgive men when they sin against you, your heavenly Father will also forgive you. But if you do not forgive men their sins, your Father will not forgive your sins."

Let Go Let God Day 7: Quit Your Worrying

Your issue will flood your head all day if you let it. You work, but your mind is on your issue; you go home—your mind is on your issue; you drive around running errands—your mind is still on your issue; you even try to sleep, but you can't. You worry all day! If you let it, your issue will control your life, sending you into a depression. You end up having that feeling in your chest where you have to take deep breaths to help you breath. You tried every which way in your mind to try to figure out how God was going to fix your situation.

Well, stop!

Challenge: Today, I challenge you to quit your worrying! Sounds difficult, but with God, you can do this. He is going to work it out.

—Psalm 55:22—

"Cast your cares on the LORD and He will sustain you; He will never let the righteous fall."

Let Go Let God Day 8: Pray

Have a talk with Jesus! Jesus knows your struggle, but He doesn't care how many times you tell Him about your situation; He still listens. He's waiting for you to reach out, but you have been silent instead of asking Him to fix it. Now, I know your saying, *"Well, if He already knows about it, then why doesn't He just fix it?"*

Sometimes, there are broken things in our house we know about it but until we call the right people to fix it then things won't get fixed. God is a man's man and he wants you to call on him so he can fix it. So as you are letting go and letting God Pray!

Challenge: Pray every day about your situation but pray a different aspect of your issue each day if it's a broken family pray for communication one day, maybe to mend it the next day, maybe for more family prayer time together the next.

—1 Thessalonians 5:17—

"Pray without ceasing."

Let Go Let God Day 9: Giants

We all have giants in our lives, strongholds that have griped us since our youth, deep-rooted issues that people may never understand. You may never share them. We put up walls and try to act like it no longer affects us, yet so often we never notice that our outward actions show our inner wounds sometimes. Even when you try to cover up a stronghold in your life, as soon as someone hits a weak spot, your poison starts to leak.

When the children of Israel spied out Jericho, they shut up their walls after the spies left because they became afraid of the intruders. They knew they were coming to knock down those walls. Sometimes, when we have strongholds, God has to send someone to knock down our walls, because if not, we will keep them up forever, and, just like Jericho, no one will come in or out (Joshua 6). We will live in what is like a house with no doors.

Challenge: Let in those people you have been trying to keep out for so long; allow yourself to be vulnerable. Let go of that stronghold you've been holding onto for so long. Allow your Jericho walls to fall. Let go and let God set you free.

—Joshua 6:20—

"So the people shouted when the priests blew with the trumpets: and it came to pass, when the people heard the sound of the trumpet, and the people shouted with a great shout, that the wall fell down flat, so that the people went up into the city, every man straight before him, and they took the city."

Let Go and Let God 10: See the Glory of God!

It's hard when you've worked hard to do something and someone takes the credit for your work. You labored for it many nights and days, yet when the final work was done, someone else gets credit for what you did. That would make anyone angry. So why do we do it to God? So often, we try to get the glory for what God does in our lives, like how you got that job but weren't qualified, how your marriage came back together after being so broken, how your family got restored, and how you conceived that baby after being barren.

Why do we always want to put our name on God's work? Sometimes, what God will do is put us in a place where He tells us to relax. Let go and let God, because He is the one who needs to get the glory. Jesus showed up when Lazarus was dead for four days (John 11). Mary and Martha probably prayed, took care of their brother when he was sick, fasted, and everything else you could imagine, but what they did never made the situation better because Lazarus still died. He died because it was a situation in which God needed to get the glory. His name was to be credited for taking a dead situation and raising it up. Jesus raised Lazarus.

Challenge: Let go and let God, and believe! Wait for Jesus to show up and raise your Lazarus in your life. You can't get the glory, because it belongs to God! Believe God for what it is that He can do in your life.

—John 11:40—

"Jesus saith unto her, Said I not unto thee, that, if thou wouldest believe, thou shouldest see the glory of God?"

Let Go Let God Day 11: Barren

Sarah wanted her baby so badly. Have you ever wanted something so much that you'd do anything for it? Sarah did; she even pushed her husband into the hands of another woman and they had a child together. Rachel told her husband, *"Give me a child, lest I die."* She would rather die than not have a child. Hannah prayed so hard that the priest thought she was drunk; she just wanted a baby, so she vowed her son to the Lord just to have him. Have you ever just wanted something so badly in your life that you were willing to do or give up anything just so you could have it? What is that thing?

Challenge: God is the only giver of life, yet sometimes, God won't let us have certain things in our life right away because we are not prepared for them. Let go of what it is that you yearn for so bad and allow God to prepare for it! Why would you want something you're not prepared for?

—Ephesians 2:10—

"For we are his workmanship, created in Christ Jesus unto good works, which God hath before ordained that we should walk in them."

Let Go Let God Day 12: Giving Up

Have you ever wanted to just give up? Your circumstance has just been so hard. Elijah prayed for no rain, and for 3 ½ years, it did not rain. Everyone who didn't see the rain suffered from famine and drought. When hard times come in our lives, we feel like giving up. We feel like we cannot make it because it's like a famine in our life, a lack of hope, a lack of something we feel we need. Although it didn't rain for 3 ½ years, Elijah and others around him survived the famine and drought. God showed up one day and told Elijah to go to Ahab (1 Kings 18) and tell him that He was going to send rain! Wait for God to send the rain!

Challenge: Look back at other situations in your life that you never thought you would make it through, but you did, and challenge yourself to keep moving forward. Trouble doesn't last always, and neither do famines in your life!

—Galatians 6:9—

"And let us not be weary in well doing: for in due season we shall reap, if we faint not."

Let Go Let God Day 13: Bitterness

Call me Mara for the Lord has dealt with me bitterly! Have you ever been so mad at the issues in your life? Have you ever felt like God has just dealt with you bitterly? Maybe you felt like the situations in your life have just caused you to turn bitter. People have betrayed your trust; life has just rubbed you the wrong way. You can't take it anymore; you just have a bitter taste in your mouth. Sometimes, when we become bitter, we push those who are meant to be in our life out of the way. Naomi almost pushed Ruth out of her life when Ruth was going to be used to help change her life. Who or what is your Ruth?

Challenge: Allow God to use certain people to help you get to the next place in your life so that he can restore life back to your life.

—Ruth 1:20—

"And she said unto them, Call me not Naomi, call me Mara: for the Almighty hath dealt very bitterly with me."

Let Go Let God Day 14: The Pit Stops to the Palace

You would never think that Joseph going through what he went through would lead him right to the place God wanted him. He went from the pit, to slavery, to jail, and finally to the palace. We often think that God has forgotten us, especially on our pit stops to where it is He showed us. Joseph literally ended up in a pit.

God will never give someone a vision for his/her life and not fulfill His vision. He told Adam and Eve after they sinned in the garden that He would send a Savior (Genesis 3:15). Then His word became flesh (John 1). It was no longer just words, but it came to life. It will no longer just be a vision God gave you, but it comes to life. It will manifest! Joseph impacted someone's life at each pit stop he made. So what if you may have to make a couple of pit stops on the way? Let go and let God have His way in your life.

Challenge: What are you doing for God while waiting for Him to bring you from your pit stops to the palace? At each pit stop in your life, impact someone else's life!

—Habakkuk 2:3—

"For the vision is yet for an appointed time; but at the end it will speak, and it will not lie. Though it tarries, wait for it, because it will surely come; it will not tarry."

Let Go Let God Day 15: Pride

Humility is something a lot of us don't have, while pride is something far more common. In society, it seems like everyone wants to be a big shot. *"I got this, God; I can take care of the situation all by myself."* Many have this attitude; they think they can do everything all alone and end up making a mess out of their own situations, and then and only then do they want to run for help. Pride is the biggest reason why a lot of people won't make it into heaven. They believe that there is nothing greater than them. Bring your head back down to size; God is bigger than you!

Often, when God is trying to reach someone by using another person, that person will try to control you, not because they are really trying to control you, but because they are trying to control God. They may stop talking to you or block your calls because they are trying to put God in a box by putting you in a box. God sees you! Look at Pharaoh in Exodus; God wanted the children of Israel free, but there was no way Pharaoh would let the people go. God got what he wanted and showed Pharaoh who was boss!

Challenge: Admit that you need help, and God can fix your situation. Ask God for help. So many people have a hard time asking for help even if it's from the Creator of the universe. Next time, do it before your situation falls apart or before God has to take matters into His own hands to make you let go. Then maybe He can help you get through it without it falling apart. Pharaoh was afraid of getting his kingdom destroyed by letting go of his slaves, but God would have caused his kingdom to fall eventually if he didn't!

—Exodus 8:32—

"And Pharaoh hardened his heart at this time also, neither would he let the people go."

Let Go Let God Day 16: Lord, My Child!

The prodigal son had everything he could ask for right at home, yet he wanted to see what the world could offer him, so he asked his father for his inheritance. Man, to be the father must have been rough. Have you ever worked hard for something only to watch someone go out and blow it away on wasteful living? We often complain about giving money to the people in front of the corner stores because we figure their habits aren't worth our money, yet what happens when it's close to home? The father just gave him what he asked for and he wasted it. Sometimes, God gives us what we ask Him for, and we waste it. The prodigal son's father just gave him what he wanted and let him go!

Challenge: Do you have a prodigal son in your life? It's time to let them go and let God have his way with them! I know it's hard, but remember, there is hope; the prodigal son came home, but also remember, he had a home to come home to!

—Luke 15:2—

"For this my son was dead, and is alive again; he was lost, and is found. And they began to be merry."

Let Go Let God Day 17: Worship

Let go, let God, and worship! God is amazing! The Bible says in John 4:24, *"God is a Spirit: and they that worship him must worship him in spirit and in truth."* Often, we go into church and sing songs, but do they really change our hearts? We listen to worship music in the car, but do we really listen to what we are singing? God's word brings life even if it's just a song, so if you're singing a song that is talking about how you need more of God, understand that God is in fact going to give you more of Him. If you're singing that you love Him more than anything, then He's going to really test you to see if you really do, especially when those songs grab a hold of you and you are singing them from your spirit. You're telling God this from the heart, *"God I worship you; I mean these words that I'm singing unto you."*

Challenge: If you're letting go and letting God, maybe you're in a situation that you just can't control, yet God has promised that He will fix it. I challenge you to worship God while you're waiting. Show Him that you love Him, you adore Him, you praise Him, and allow it to come from the heart, not something like, "Yeah, okay God, I love you," but a "YEAH, LORD, I LOVE YOU!" Do you really mean it?

—2 Samuel 6:14—

"And David danced before the Lord with all his might; and David was girded with a linen ephod."

Let Go Let God Day 18: Transitioning

Transitioning in life can be hard. You can be moving from state to state, moving from job to job, going from singleness to marriage, welcoming in a child, or God can be changing you to be who He needs you to be for the next season of your life. Whatever the case may be, transition can be hard. We often try to hold on to old things while trying to move forward at the same time, yet with any transition, we must understand that transition means change!

Abram knew a lot about this in Genesis 12. God told him to get out of his country to a place He would show him, and leave things behind. Abram didn't do that; he brought his past into his future by bringing his cousin, Lot. How many times do we bring our past into our future? How many of us bring our Lot? Abram should have let go to move forward, but obviously, it wasn't that easy. By chapter 13 of Genesis, however, God had to separate the two, because God couldn't give Abram what he wanted unless he separated from his Lot.

Challenge: Think about what your Lot is in your life and how you will separate from it in order to move forward in your life! Maybe it's your family, your marriage, or the harmful cycles of your past that you keep going back to. We can hurt ourselves as well as other people in the process. Listen to God's instructions when it comes to transitioning. If you have to leave things behind, know there is better ahead.

—Genesis 12:1—

"Now the Lord had said unto Abram, Get thee out of thy country, and from thy kindred, and from thy father's house, unto a land that I will shew thee."

Let Go Let God Day 19: Rebuild, Restore, and Revive

Broken—what a horrible word. In this world, so many people just throw away things that are broken. People don't want something they have to fix, but Jesus does! That's good news! That's why the Gospel is called the good news! A man who is perfect and holy wants broken people. Jesus wants to rebuild, restore, and revive people's lives. You may feel like there is no hope, but God can do it. Okay, so you're probably thinking, *"Well, I've been in my situation for too long."* There is still hope!

There is a woman in the Bible known as the woman with the issue of blood. She struggled with her issue for twelve years (Mark 5:25-34), and, like her, we all have issues that we struggle with for so long. With her issue, it made her unclean, so everyone left her, and no one could help her, so this woman did what any other person who needs help does—press her way to Jesus. When Jesus felt her touch Him, she was made well. He felt His power leave Him, and the disciples thought that it was just the multitudes around Him, but it was the woman with the issue of blood! So, what are you waiting for? Reach out for Jesus; touch the hem of his garment, and ask

Him to restore, revive, and rebuild your life!

Challenge: All you have to do is touch; reach out for Jesus, and He will revive, restore and rebuild your life.

—Mark 5:34—

"And he said unto her, Daughter, thy faith hath made thee whole; go in peace, and be whole of thy plague."

Let Go Let God Day 20: Help My Unbelief

"I can't believe this! Nope, no way; there is no way on Earth this can happen—maybe for someone else, but definitely not for me."

Wow, did you know that words are powerful? According to Proverbs 18:21, *"Death and life are in the power of the tongue: and they that love it shall eat the fruit thereof."* This holds to be so true; God created the world with words! God spoke and the world took form.

In Numbers 13-14, the children of Israel went to go spy out the land. The spies came back with a bad report; they never entered into the promise land. Why? It was because they spoke a negative report. How could God give them a land flowing with milk and honey if they only saw giants? They were in disbelief of what God said they could have, yet there was still hope in Joshua and Caleb. They saw what God saw and spoke what God spoke, a land flowing with milk and honey, and knew they were well able to overcome the giants in the land. Those who believed and saw the land through Gods eyes entered into the promise land. Those who had unbelief and saw the land with eyes like the world never did.

Challenge: The promises of God are yours. Do you believe that, or do you live in unbelief? Today, believe God can deliver to you what He has offered. If you can believe God, you can see it. Faith is not what you see, but what you believe (Hebrews 1:11).

—Mark 9:24—

"And straightway the father of the child cried out, and said with tears, Lord, I believe; help thou mine unbelief."

Let Go Let God Day 21: Let Go, and Let God Love You!

Everyone wants to be loved. There is not one person on this planet who doesn't want to be loved, yet so many people look for love in men or women, friends, family, or a spouse. We all have that in common, yet we often find ourselves filling our life with people or things that can't fill our voids. This is because God is the only one who can love you the way that you need to be loved.

In John 4, there is a woman from Samaria who was outcasted because, well, let's just say the men of the town knew her name. She had six husbands, and the man she was with at the time was not her husband. She had been looking for love for a very long time. There was then a day that she went to a well, and she found Jesus sitting there. When she got there, she found out that she was a very thirsty woman (Now men can be thirsty too, but that's not the point). The point is that she found only Jesus could quench her thirst for love. To quote John 4:13-14, *"Jesus answered and said unto her, Whosoever drinketh of this water shall thirst again: But whosoever drinketh of the water that I shall give him shall never thirst; but the water that I shall give him shall be in him a well of water springing up into everlasting life."*

Challenge: God loves you, and He wants to quench your thirst for love. Today, ask God to fill you with His love, teach you how to love like Him, and understand how great His love is.

—1 John 4:8—

"He that loveth not knoweth not God; for God is love."

Let Go Let God Day 22: Seek Ye First the Kingdom of God

"Life is about me; well God, can you help me? Lord, do you see me? Do you see my needs? Me, me, me!"

Me, oh, me, oh, my, it sounds like you've got a case of the "me's," the "my's," and the "mine's!" We often dwell on our circumstances because we are always worried about ourselves. This is why so many people have depression. *"My life is so bad; do you see what just happened to me? Nobody else's life is like this but mine."* Thinking about yourself all day is not healthy! God never sits around and thinks about Himself all day because if He did, there would be so much more chaos going on in this world than there already is. What God does do is think about the needs of others.

Challenge: When is the last time you went out and told someone about Jesus? Today is that day! Tell someone about Jesus and what He did for you in your life!

—Matthew 6:33—

"But seek ye first the kingdom of God, and his righteousness; and all these things shall be added unto you."

Let Go Let God Day 23: Mourning

We have all been there; we've had a situation in our lives that we knew God could keep from falling apart, keep from dying. He's God; we know what He can do. Martha and Mary knew this very well; they knew Jesus could save their brother Lazarus even in his sick state with such little life left in him, but Jesus never came. Jesus never showed up. You start wondering, *"Where you are Lord? Do you hear me? Do you see my pain? I know you can fix this, so please come and fix it!"*

Sometimes, God never shows up like we would like, but He does have a plan. David prayed and fasted when his son was about to die, yet God never showed up. David, however, found comfort knowing his child would be in heaven with God. Know that when we are going through moments of sorrow and pain, there is comfort in God. Even Jesus wept in John 11 when He was told that Lazarus was buried in the tomb. It's okay to be upset; just don't stay there for too long. Let go, and let God give you peace. You won't always get your loved ones back, but if you ask, God can give you the comfort that you need to get through. You just have to ask!

Challenge: Take a balloon and write a letter to the person you lost; tie it on the balloon and let it go. Allow God to take control!

—Psalm 147:3—

"He healeth the broken in heart, and bindeth up their wounds."

Let Go Let God Day 24: Direction

Have you ever felt lost, out of place, stuck, or maybe seeking direction? Have you ever felt like you're going in circles? It's like a repeated cycle, and at this point, you just want to get to a destination. You don't care where it is; you just want to be anywhere but where you are. Some of us don't even have a sense of direction as far as what God wants for our lives. We are too busy wandering in life trying to find ourselves.

The children of Israel wandered in the wilderness for forty years. This was a result of their disbelief that God had a place for them, a promised land. He had a plan for their lives, a destination for them to reach, yet they never believed. That is a long time to live without really having a destination to reach. Imagine them waiting to escape the wilderness year after year, never really knowing where they were going. Some of them were never going to get out and see the promised land, but instead just walked around aimlessly. We too sometimes walk around in life with no direction for ourselves.

Challenge: God has a plan for your life! Have you ever asked him what His plan for your life is? Have you ever asked him, *"Lord, am I going in the wrong direction? I have been wandering around for a while, but now I want a destination!"*

—Jeremiah 29:11—

"For I know the thoughts that I think toward you, saith the Lord, thoughts of peace, and not of evil, to give you an expected end."

Let Go Let God Day 25: Contentment

We always want the next best thing, and then once we have it, we want the next best thing, and then when we have that, we want the next best thing, never really being content with that which we already have but out longing for more. We do it with our homes, our kids, our relationships, our jobs, the places we are at in life, and material things. We never have enough, and we are always longing for more. Have you ever really sat down and looked at the definition of contentment?

Contentment (noun): A state of happiness and satisfaction.

Challenge: Let go, and let God! Have you learned to be content at any place in life that you're in? Start enjoying your life in whatever situation you're in.

—Philippians 4:11-12—

"Not that I speak in respect of want: for I have learned, in whatsoever state I am, therewith to be content. I know both how to be abased, and I know how to abound: everywhere and in all things I am instructed both to be full and to be hungry, both to abound and to suffer need."

Let Go Let God Day 26: Build Your House

"Lord, my family is out of control!"

Is God your foundation, or have you built your house on other things like money and material possessions? That stuff will all one day fade away, and you will then be left with nothing but broken pieces to pick up. Many people don't understand that those things cannot mend a broken family, but God can.

God told Hosea to marry a prostitute, and she went out and ran to the world. She had everything she needed at home, but it was never good enough. Now, you're probably saying, *"Well, Hosea was founded on God, but his house broke."* Yes, it did, but in the end, Hosea got his wife back because the world didn't love her. Hosea was grounded in the Lord and trusted the Lord with his situation with his family, and by the end they came back together!

Challenge: Trust the Lord with your family! Get a notebook and pen, then sit down and pray. Ask God to restore your family and reveal what He would like you to do to help. Things can change; Noah's family was saved from the flood!

—Genesis 6:14—

"Make thee an ark of gopher wood; rooms shalt thou make in the ark, and shalt pitch it within and without with pitch."

Let Go Let God Day 27: Egypt

The world is a rough place. There are so many people in life living in sin, and they think it's normal. They believe that they can do whatever they want, but they don't want to face the consequences. Those that live this way don't think they should have to answer for what people describe as "little sin."

"Well, my sin's not as bad as their sin."

Sorry to break it to you, but sin is sin no matter how you put it. Romans 3:23 states that *"all have sinned, and come short of the glory of God."* That should take a load off of everyone's back; everyone has sinned. There is not one perfect person, yet there is a perfect God, and that's why He sent us His perfect holy son, Jesus.

The children of Israel were enslaved in Egypt, and Pharaoh wouldn't let them go. God sent all type of plagues there until Pharaoh finally let them go. Pharaoh is like our sin; it doesn't want to let us go, and if we aren't careful, we will get comfortable in Egypt, comfortable in our bondage, and then it just becomes normal living to us. Yes, we are all sinners, but we don't have to be enslaved to our sin. We all have a sin or sins we struggle with, but we can be free. God freed the children of Israel from their bondage.

Challenge: Let go, and let God free you from your sin. Have you given your life to Jesus? If you haven't, then today is the day! Maybe you're saved, but you are struggling with certain sins; well, allow God to work with you to help set you free.

—Romans 6:6—

"Knowing this, that our old man is crucified with him, that the body of sin might be destroyed, that henceforth we should not serve sin."

Let Go Let God Day 28: Behold I Do a New Thing

Change is here! God is doing a new thing in your life because you let go and you let God. You are finally ready for what it is that God has for you in your life. The children of Israel finally got their promise because they changed their way of thinking from disbelief to belief! It is time for what it is that God has for you. I know it's probably too good to be true, but don't die right at the edge of the Jordan! Though the children of Israel still had to fight some battles in the promise land, it didn't matter. They understood that the promise land belonged to them. In Joshua 1, God keeps telling Joshua to be strong and courageous. Why do you think that is? It's because God is strong and courageous; He was going to win every battle for them as long as they did what God wanted them to do in obedience. Joshua 1:6 says to, *"be strong and of a good courage: for unto this people shalt thou divide for an inheritance the land, which I swear unto their fathers to give them."*

Challenge: Be strong and courageous! Let go, and let God fight your battle for you! You have already won; the victory is yours, so stand up and act like it!

—Isaiah 43:18-19—

“Remember ye not the former things, neither consider the things of old. Behold, I will do a new thing; now it shall spring forth; shall ye not know it? I will even make a way in the wilderness, and rivers in the desert.”

Let Go Let God Day 29: Cheerfully Give

A lot of us let money run our lives. Material things control the media like it's nobody's business. We will often give our money for everything else but won't use it for God's purpose. There is all something that we need to learn, and for many this is a struggle. What we must learn is how to trust God with our money. God is a provider, and He will provide all your needs for you.

The rich young ruler had everything that the world had to offer him, yet the one thing he didn't have was Jesus. Yes, he was a good man, and he kept the law, but that doesn't mean anything if you don't have Jesus. Jesus told him to leave everything he had, give and sell to the poor, take up his cross, and follow Him, yet the man refused; he choose his material possessions and wealth over Jesus.

Challenge: Today, I challenge you to go out and cheerfully do something for a random person just to be a blessing. Give. You may not have much to give but a cheerful, encouraging word, maybe your time to listen, a gift, or maybe money; think outside of the box. Make it fun and creative!

—2 Corinthians 9:7—

"Every man according as he purposeth in his heart, so let him give; not grudgingly, or of necessity: for God loveth a cheerful giver."

Let Go Let God Day 30: New Covenant

God made a covenant with Noah before the flood, and he made a new covenant with Noah after the flood. The new covenant came with a promise rainbow stating that what just happened in his life would never happen again (Genesis 7-9). What God is saying to you is that you will never have to go through what you just went through again. Other storms may come, but just as He got you through this last one on your ark, He will get you through the next storm that may come. You have let go and let God! You have allowed him to take over your life and control what it is that He wanted to take control of. The storms may have come, and you may have gotten a little beat up along the way, but you survived! Noah got to start anew in a new land! Your dove with its olive branch has returned, and peace is finally here!

Challenge: Maybe you have done things in your life that have shaken up the lives of others. Some of you may not be able to change the issue, but some you can make it better. You are fresh and new, so now it's time to start taking the actions you have learned and start anew!

—Jeremiah 31:31—

"Behold, the days come, saith the Lord, that I will make a new covenant with the house of Israel, and with the house of Judah."

Let Go Let God Day 31: It Is Finished!

It can be hard to allow God to be God in your life and take control. It feels like you have been going on a ride that you cannot control. Jesus knew He had to die on the cross, but He still let go and let God have His way. The Bible says in John 19:30, *"When Jesus therefore had received the vinegar, he said, it is finished: and he bowed his head, and gave up the ghost."* Jesus willingly gave up the ghost! He didn't have to die on the cross, but He chose to. Jesus chose the will of His father so that we could be reconciled back to God, yet what makes Jesus Lord is that He rose back up from the dead! Maybe you have let go and let God, and your life has fallen apart. It was only because He was trying to get you to die to yourself, but He is going to raise you back up! Don't stay dead, but live! Rise up!

Challenge: Allow God to raise you up to the place where He has called you to be! You can't do it, but God can. Jesus defeated the grave; now it's time to get out of the grave in your life!

—Acts 1:9—

"And when he had spoken these things, while they beheld, he was taken up; and a cloud received him out of their sight."

www.ingramcontent.com/pod-product-compliance
Ingram Content Group UK Ltd.
Pitfield, Milton Keynes, MK11 3LW, UK
UKHW020230250726
13967UKWH00001B/286

9 781304 367112